Around 1800, a sperm whale was born that was destined to become legend. His first recorded attack against a whaleboat occurred in 1810. He would go on to wage more than 100 battles with whalers.

Mocha Dick's physical description and accomplishments are well documented. According to the men who hunted him, he was one of the largest, most powerful, and most cunning of all sperm whales. Often referred to as "the White Whale of the Pacific," his place in sea lore was so prominent that Mocha Dick became the inspiration for the great white whale in Herman Melville's 1851 novel *Moby-Dick*.

This is the story of MOCHA DICK.

For my editor, Aaron—a sharp eye, a keen ear, and a trusted friend to fine language. –BJH
For my wife Leann. –RE

Text copyright © 2014 Brian J. Heinz / Illustrations copyright © 2014 Randall Enos / Designed by Rita Marshall
Edited by Aaron Frisch / Published in 2014 by Creative Editions / P.O. Box 227, Mankato, MN 56002 USA
Creative Editions is an imprint of The Creative Company / All rights reserved. No part of the contents of
this book may be reproduced by any means without the written permission of the publisher. / Printed in China
Library of Congress Cataloging-in-Publication Data / Heinz, Brian J. / Mocha Dick: the legend and fury
by Brian Heinz; illustrated by Randall Enos. / Summary: The original great white whale, first spied off the coast
of Chile in 1810, becomes a prime target for whalers as he thrashes about the Pacific and achieves legendary status.
ISBN 978-1-56846-242-4 / 1. Sperm whale—Juvenile fiction. [1. Sperm whale—Fiction. 2. Whales—Fiction.
3. Whaling—Fiction.] I. Enos, Randall, illustrator. II. Title. / PZ10.3.H31765Moc 2014 / [Fic]—dc23 / 2013040661
First Edition 9 8 7 6 5 4 3 2 1

MOCHA DICK: THE LEGEND AND FURY

by Brian Heinz

illustrated by Randall Enos

Creative Editions

OFF

the coast of Chile, waters churned
around the sun-soaked island of Mocha.
Shrieking seabirds hovered
above the waves.

THE OCEAN'S surface exploded as the sperm

whale breached skyward. Then, his seventy feet of majesty slammed onto the

sea, sending up fountains of spume. Droplets fell like jewels upon his back. His

flukes hammered the surface like a cannon shot.

AS he vented his lungs in a white plume, the whale was unaware that each blow beckoned a tall wooden ship. He could not know of the excitement he aroused in the men on the ship's deck.

AS the whale plunged to the depths, three boats cut through the waves.

The whale surfaced and expelled hot breath in a dramatic *Whoosh*.

"He blows!" the mate at the steering oar cried. "Lay your backs into those oars!"

The peaceful giant cruised ahead, but the lead boat was soon upon him.

THE HARPOONER raised his weapon.

"Let the iron fly!"

The wooden shaft cut through the air. The iron barb punctured thick skin. In a rush of searing pain, the whale surged forward. The rope sprung tight as a bowstring, and the boat whisked over the waves in tow behind the great creature.

THE WHALE agonized against the twisting iron. In

defense, he turned in a shallow dive. The line went slack. The boat bobbed like a cork. Sailors sat bewildered.

Suddenly, the whale burst through the waves, his jaws gnashing in the foam. One sweep of his flukes hurled the craft high into the air, spilling the crew into the sea. Twenty-six pairs of teeth as long as a man's hand clamped down on the boat. The huge head shook savagely until only splinters remained. Then the whale disappeared in the twilight. The remaining boats plucked up their comrades and rowed briskly to their whaler. Some men sat stone-faced. Some shook.

"Did you see him?" asked one. "As pale as a ghost and as big as the ship's hull."

"With a cavern for a mouth," added another. "And what about that scar?"

THE CREW nodded. Indeed, a white scar ran eight feet across the whale's brow.

"He needs a name, a whale like that," said an oarsman.

The second mate glanced back at the island of Mocha. "He is Mocha Dick."

Summer passed. Word spread quickly of the spectacular whale. Captains at
the rails lifted speaking trumpets to hail passing ships. "Any word from
Mocha Dick?"

IN warm Pacific waters, Mocha Dick was sighted again. A ship's boats gave chase. A muscled arm hurled a harpoon. The barb sliced the whale's back and bounced into the sea. Mocha Dick sent up a spout that roared like a geyser, then sounded.

The boats drifted in circles for a full hour. The ship's lanterns glowed in the distance. A sailor broke the silence. "What whale dives, never to rise again?" Three leagues away, Mocha Dick surfaced, the soft sea nursing his wound.

Mocha Dick migrated alone, over countless Pacific miles, avoiding confrontations with man, seeking his peace. Whalers often gave chase, but he eluded the sting of the harpoon.

IN the middle of the ocean, the 238-ton *Essex*, a Nantucket whaler under furled sails, cooked down blubber to a fine and valuable oil. The blazing furnace of her try works spewed black smoke and the stench of burning flesh.

MOCHA DICK spouted long and tall. Water flew from the oar blades as a boat approached and rode onto the whale's back. The mate planted a harpoon. Mocha Dick rose like an island and walloped a hole in the boat's side before sounding.

THE CREW stripped off clothing to halt the invading

seawater as they limped back to the *Essex*.

But in the depths, an intelligence awakened in the whale. His past wounds, and this fresh pain, lit a fire. Mocha Dick became the hunter.

Aboard the *Essex*, the ship's carpenter looked to windward. "Oh, lads. He's comin' for us."

MOCHA DICK drove in at twenty knots, and 90,000 pounds of seething fury struck the port bow, caving in the frames. Men were tossed about like rag dolls. Rigging swung wildly overhead, and water rushed into the belly of the ship.

MOCHA DICK passed beneath the ship, brushing

her keel. Then, he turned and crushed her starboard quarter. The *Essex* settled low in the water and rolled onto her side. Mocha Dick left his enemies to their fates.

Years fell from calendars. Not an evening passed that Mocha Dick's name was not whispered by sailors curled in their bunks. In the dark, they dreamed of boiling him down for the oil that would light their lamps and candles.

IN the South Pacific, Mocha Dick encountered the stout Russian whaler *Serepta*. Two boat crews struggled against their oars towing a whale's carcass, unaware of the beast below. As he erupted from the depths, faces paled at the sight of the telltale scar. Mocha Dick battered the first boat with fluke and fin, sending sailors to the bottoms, then turned for the second. The terrified crew cut their lines and hailed their ship.

On deck, a seaman turned to the vessel's master. "Shall we take him on, sir?"

The master looked upon Mocha Dick. "No," he said. "Better to lose a whale than a ship."

The *Serepta* shook out her sails and made off. Mocha Dick circled the dead whale's body, as if keeping vigil.

The whalers continued to come—Yankees, Russians, Dutch, English, and Swedes, all flying their proud flags. For another year, Mocha Dick evaded battle.

IT was a cold autumn day when Mocha Dick surfaced behind a lumber schooner bound for the Japanese coast. Charging, he bashed in her stern.

Three whale ships came to the crippled schooner's aid, and the captains conspired to sail in company against Mocha Dick.

MOCHA DICK breached skyward, as if to

say, *I am here*.

Pulleys squealed as six boats dropped to the sea like spiders from
their webs.

A HARPOON struck Mocha Dick behind the head. The whale surged briefly forward, then stopped. He wheezed. He twitched. Then, he lay as if dead. When the boats drew close, Mocha Dick exploded to life. Dragging one boat in his wake, he crushed a second and snatched the third in his jaws, reducing it to kindling. Two men tumbled into the mouth and were swallowed whole. The remaining boats raced for the closest ship and clambered aboard as Mocha Dick sounded.

Mocha Dick could find no peace. He battled and he triumphed, but his many victories came at great cost. Six teeth were shattered, one eye made blind. His flesh carried the rusting heads of nineteen harpoons. Mocha Dick wearied of the game, but the game was not ended.

A Swedish lookout bellowed, "He blows! Dead ahead and all alone!"

A harpoon flew and cut Mocha Dick to the bone.

MOCHA DICK leaped. His flukes caught the steering oar, and the craft rose on its end. The bow plunged under the waves as sailors clung to their seats. But Mocha Dick stopped short of swamping the boat. With desperate gasps for air, he lay quivering at the surface.

THE MATE drove a flashing spade into the narrows of the whale's tail, crippling the flukes. Mocha Dick made a final lunge, but his strength ebbed away. His spirit was broken. Though the sun shone as brightly as it did in his youth, on that day so long ago in the seas of Mocha Island, a great emptiness settled over the endless miles of restless water.

A lance sank in behind Mocha Dick's flipper, finding his lungs. The water boiled as the great whale thrashed in circles, clacking his teeth. Then, the jaws stopped.

The great whale rolled onto his side. Mocha Dick finally found his peace.

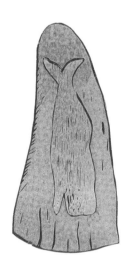

EPITAPH

Beware, ye sailors in wooden ships, borne by wind and sail,

Who trespass into the fearful realm of this cunning ghost-white whale.

For oft a seasoned seaman, though he may be brave and quick,

Was sent to rot on the ocean's floor by the mighty Mocha Dick.